Creative Education

ANIMALS & PLANTS

On The Cover:
An Ancient Forest and Giant Dragonfly.
The first living things were plants.
Animals came later—and they have
always depended on plants for food.
Cover Art by Walter Stuart.

Published by Creative Education, Inc., 123 South Broad Street, Mankato, Minnesota 56001

Printed by permission of Wildlife Education, Ltd.

ISBN 0-88682-389-7

Created and written by
John Bonnett Wexo

Chief Artist
Walter Stuart

Senior Art Consultant
Mark Hallett

Design Consultant
Eldon Paul Slick

Production Art Director
Maurene Mongan

Production Artists
Bob Meyer
Fiona King
Hildago Ruiz

Photo Staff
Renee C. Burch
Katharine Boskoff

Publisher
Kenneth Kitson

Associate Publisher
Ray W. Ehlers

ANIMALS & PLANTS

This Volume is Dedicated To: Alexander and Noah Wexo, my sons, who have both made me proud of their talents and their achievements.

Art Credits

Pages Eight and Nine: John Francis; **Pages Ten and Eleven:** John Francis; **Page Eleven: Upper Right, Middle Right, and Lower Right:** Walter Stuart; **Pages Twelve and Thirteen:** John Francis; **Pages Fourteen and Fifteen:** John Francis; **Pages Sixteen and Seventeen:** John Francis; **Pages Eighteen and Nineteen:** John Francis; **Page Twenty: Middle Right,** Walter Stuart; **Pages Twenty and Twenty-one:** John Francis; **Page Twenty-one: Lower Right,** Walter Stuart; **Pages Twenty-two and Twenty-three: Background,** Timothy Hayward; **Figures,** Chuck Byron, Jr.

Photographic Credits

Pages Six and Seven: L. S. Stepanowicz *(Bruce Coleman, Inc.)*; **Page Nine: Upper Right,** D. Jorgenson *(Tom Stack & Assoc.)*; **Lower Right and Far Lower Right,** D. Jorgenson *(Tom Stack & Assoc.)*; **Page Fifteen: Lower Right,** Biophoto Assoc./Science Source *(Photo Researchers)*.

Creative Education would like to thank Wildlife Education, Ltd., for granting them the right to print and distribute this hardbound edition.

Contents

After millions of years, the water was full of many kinds of cells . . .

BOOK THREE

Animals & Plants

As you have seen, the first living things on earth were *simple*—just cells that could make copies of themselves. For a long time, life remained at this simple stage. But then, *more complicated living things* began to develop. First, plants evolved that could make their own food. Then, animals came along that could eat plants. And finally, animals evolved that could eat other animals. Life became more and more complicated . . .

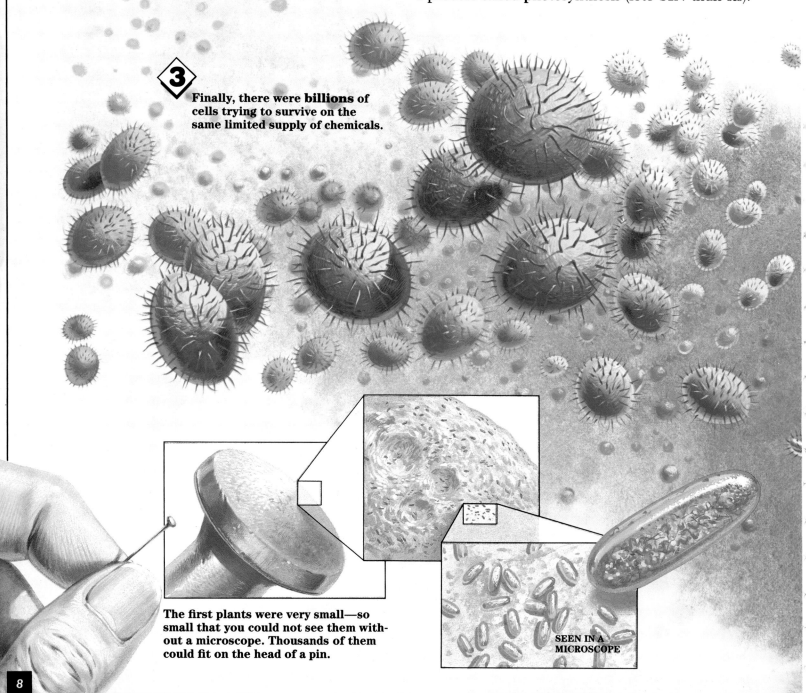

1 To start with, there were only a few simple cells and lots of chemicals for them to eat. The primitive cells didn't have any mouths, so they took in their food directly through their "skins"— their **cell membranes** (MEM-brains).

2 As time passed, the cells thrived on the chemicals and the number of cells grew. There were **more and more cells** eating the same supply of food.

3 Finally, there were **billions** of cells trying to survive on the same limited supply of chemicals.

The first living things were simple cells. They were very small and they floated in the water. To stay alive, these first cells needed food. And they found it in the water around them.

To begin with, they fed on chemicals that were dissolved in the oceans as the earth was being formed. But the supply of these chemicals was limited—so the number of cells that could feed on them was limited. **Life almost got stuck** at a very simple stage because **there wasn't enough food.**

Luckily, the first plants evolved, and they could **make food** out of materials that were very common in the oceans. To make food, they used a process called **photosynthesis** (foto-SIN-thuh-sis).

The first plants were very small—so small that you could not see them without a microscope. Thousands of them could fit on the head of a pin.

SEEN IN A MICROSCOPE

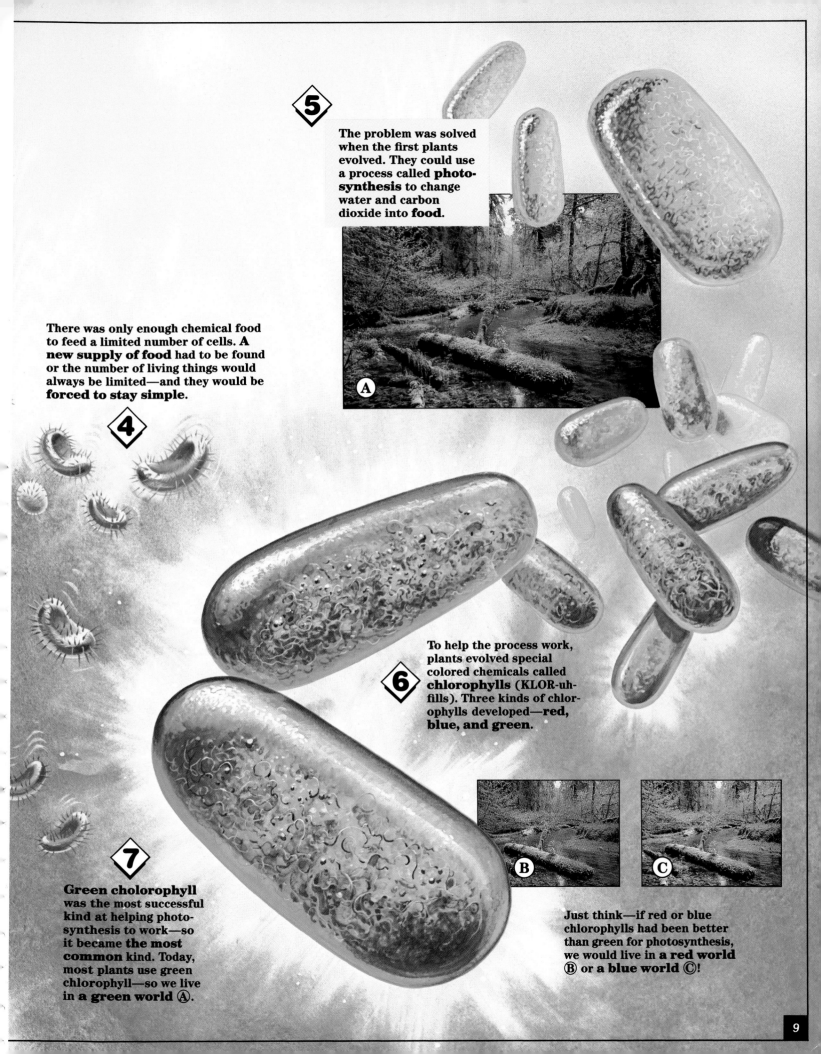

⑤

The problem was solved when the first plants evolved. They could use a process called **photosynthesis** to change water and carbon dioxide into **food.**

Ⓐ

There was only enough chemical food to feed a limited number of cells. **A new supply of food** had to be found or the number of living things would always be limited—and they would be **forced to stay simple.**

④

⑥

To help the process work, plants evolved special colored chemicals called **chlorophylls** (KLOR-uh-fills). Three kinds of chlorophylls developed—**red, blue, and green.**

Ⓑ   Ⓒ

⑦

Green cholorophyll was the most successful kind at helping photosynthesis to work—so it became **the most common** kind. Today, most plants use green chlorophyll—so we live in **a green world** Ⓐ.

Just think—if red or blue chlorophylls had been better than green for photosynthesis, we would live in **a red world** Ⓑ or **a blue world** Ⓒ!

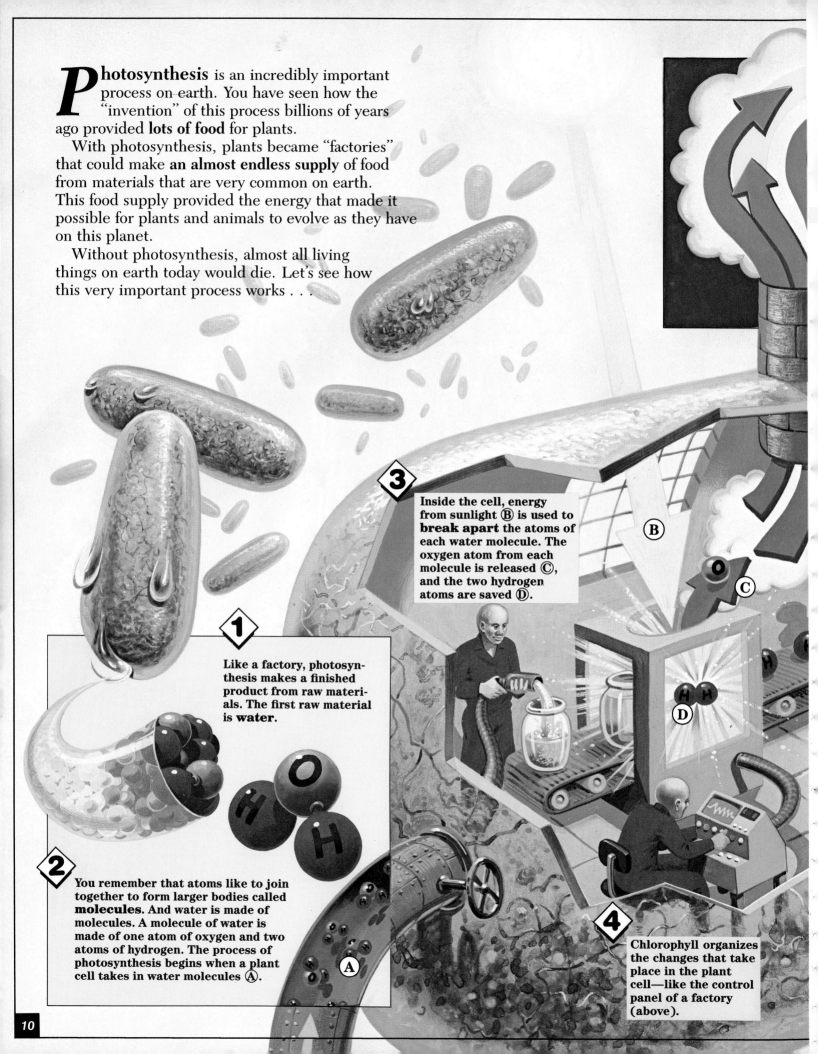

Photosynthesis is an incredibly important process on earth. You have seen how the "invention" of this process billions of years ago provided **lots of food** for plants.

With photosynthesis, plants became "factories" that could make **an almost endless supply** of food from materials that are very common on earth. This food supply provided the energy that made it possible for plants and animals to evolve as they have on this planet.

Without photosynthesis, almost all living things on earth today would die. Let's see how this very important process works . . .

3 Inside the cell, energy from sunlight Ⓑ is used to **break apart** the atoms of each water molecule. The oxygen atom from each molecule is released Ⓒ, and the two hydrogen atoms are saved Ⓓ.

1 Like a factory, photosynthesis makes a finished product from raw materials. The first raw material is **water**.

2 You remember that atoms like to join together to form larger bodies called **molecules**. And water is made of molecules. A molecule of water is made of one atom of oxygen and two atoms of hydrogen. The process of photosynthesis begins when a plant cell takes in water molecules Ⓐ.

4 Chlorophyll organizes the changes that take place in the plant cell—like the control panel of a factory (above).

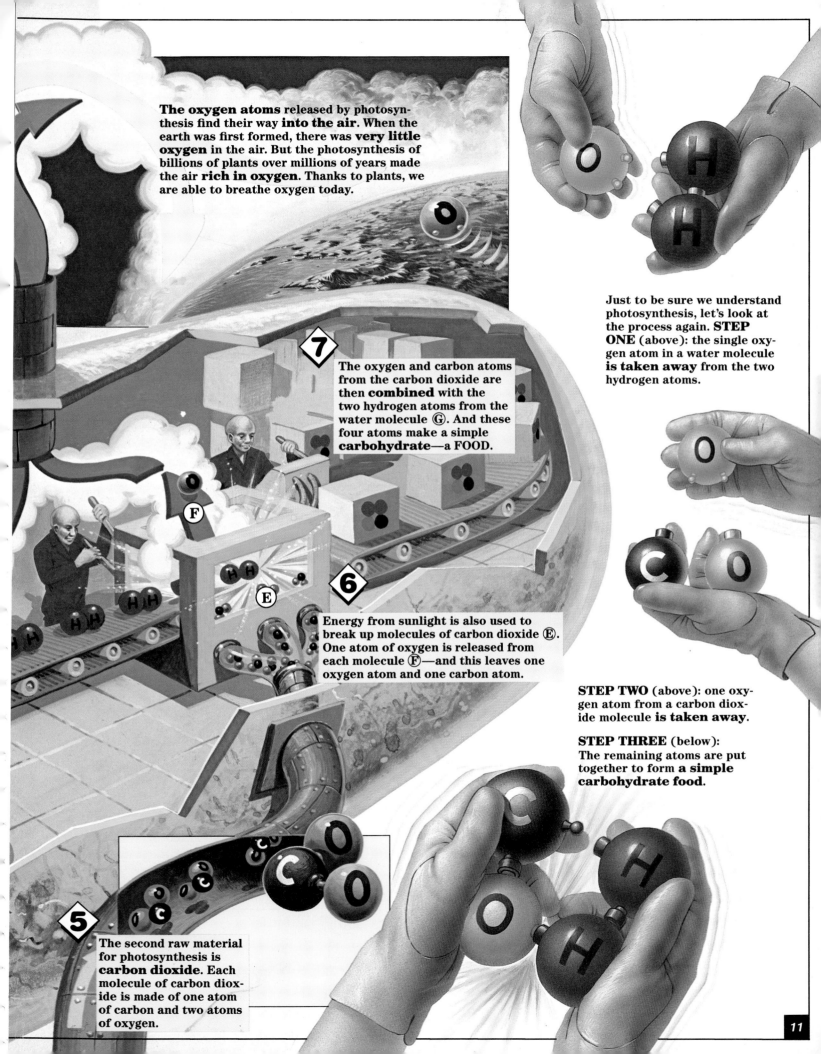

The **oxygen atoms** released by photosynthesis find their way **into the air**. When the earth was first formed, there was **very little oxygen** in the air. But the photosynthesis of billions of plants over millions of years made the air **rich in oxygen**. Thanks to plants, we are able to breathe oxygen today.

⑦ The oxygen and carbon atoms from the carbon dioxide are then **combined** with the two hydrogen atoms from the water molecule ⑥. And these four atoms make a simple **carbohydrate—a FOOD.**

⑥ Energy from sunlight is also used to break up molecules of carbon dioxide Ⓔ. One atom of oxygen is released from each molecule Ⓕ—and this leaves one oxygen atom and one carbon atom.

⑤ The second raw material for photosynthesis is **carbon dioxide**. Each molecule of carbon dioxide is made of one atom of carbon and two atoms of oxygen.

Just to be sure we understand photosynthesis, let's look at the process again. **STEP ONE** (above): the single oxygen atom in a water molecule **is taken away** from the two hydrogen atoms.

STEP TWO (above): one oxygen atom from a carbon dioxide molecule **is taken away.**

STEP THREE (below): The remaining atoms are put together to form **a simple carbohydrate food.**

11

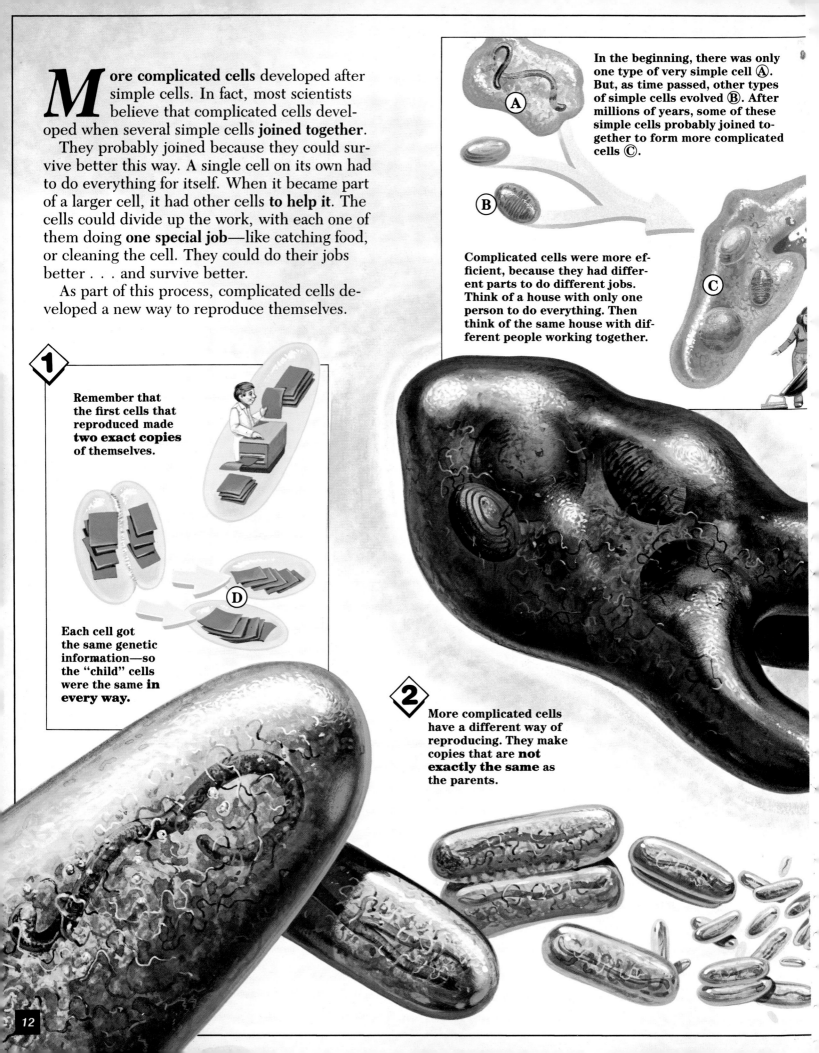

More complicated cells developed after simple cells. In fact, most scientists believe that complicated cells developed when several simple cells **joined together**.

They probably joined because they could survive better this way. A single cell on its own had to do everything for itself. When it became part of a larger cell, it had other cells **to help it**. The cells could divide up the work, with each one of them doing **one special job**—like catching food, or cleaning the cell. They could do their jobs better . . . and survive better.

As part of this process, complicated cells developed a new way to reproduce themselves.

In the beginning, there was only one type of very simple cell Ⓐ. But, as time passed, other types of simple cells evolved Ⓑ. After millions of years, some of these simple cells probably joined together to form more complicated cells Ⓒ.

Complicated cells were more efficient, because they had different parts to do different jobs. Think of a house with only one person to do everything. Then think of the same house with different people working together.

1

Remember that the first cells that reproduced made **two exact copies** of themselves.

Each cell got the same genetic information—so the "child" cells were the same **in every way**.

2

More complicated cells have a different way of reproducing. They make copies that are **not exactly the same** as the parents.

12

5 After that, each cell **combines** the half of its own information with the half it has received. Then it **makes two copies** of this **combined information** Ⓖ.

4 The cells join, and each gives **one half** of its copied information to the other Ⓕ.

3 In the new process of reproduction, **two cells get together**—the "mother" and "father" cells. Each cell makes **one copy** of its genetic information Ⓔ.

6 Then the cell splits into two new cells Ⓗ. Each new cell gets **a combination of genetic information** from its "mother" and "father."

7 As you know, this method of making copies is **good for evolution**. Animals can change faster this way—and that's exactly what happened. After this new method was "invented," evolution started to **move faster**.

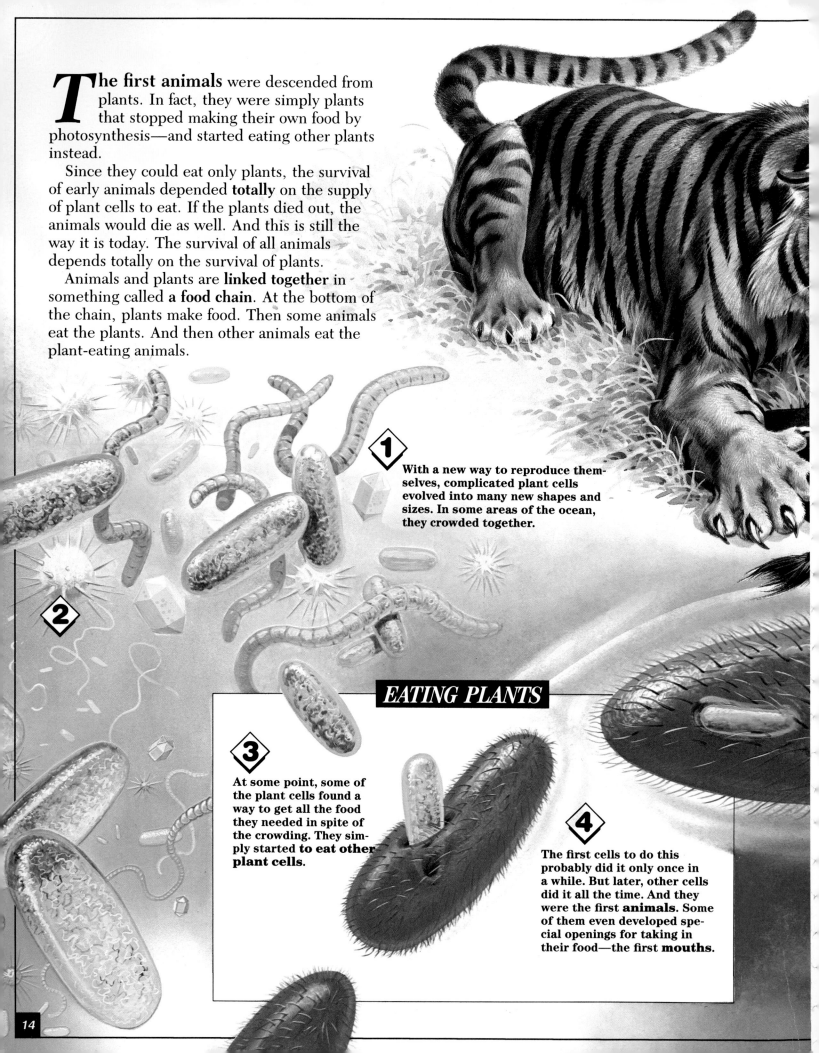

The first animals were descended from plants. In fact, they were simply plants that stopped making their own food by photosynthesis—and started eating other plants instead.

Since they could eat only plants, the survival of early animals depended **totally** on the supply of plant cells to eat. If the plants died out, the animals would die as well. And this is still the way it is today. The survival of all animals depends totally on the survival of plants.

Animals and plants are **linked together** in something called **a food chain**. At the bottom of the chain, plants make food. Then some animals eat the plants. And then other animals eat the plant-eating animals.

1 With a new way to reproduce themselves, complicated plant cells evolved into many new shapes and sizes. In some areas of the ocean, they crowded together.

2

EATING PLANTS

3 At some point, some of the plant cells found a way to get all the food they needed in spite of the crowding. They simply started **to eat other plant cells.**

4 The first cells to do this probably did it only once in a while. But later, other cells did it all the time. And they were the first **animals**. Some of them even developed special openings for taking in their food—the first **mouths.**

Many of the animals and plants that you can see in the world today are larger than the first animals and plants. But they are still part of the same kind of food chain.

FOOD CHAINS

At the top of the chain are **the predators** Ⓐ. They eat mostly meat from other animals—so they are called **carnivores** (CAR-nuh-vorz), which means "meat-eaters." In the middle of the chain are animals that eat mostly plants Ⓑ. They are called **herbivores** (URB-uh-vorz), which means "plant-eaters."

At the bottom of the food chain are the plants Ⓒ. They are still the only living things that can make their own food by photosynthesis. They don't need animals—but animals certainly need them.

EATING MEAT

5 After a time, other cells evolved that ate the plant-eating cells. These were the first **predators**. All of this happened more than two billion years ago.

Today, the big predator cells still eat the smaller cells—as they have for millions of years.

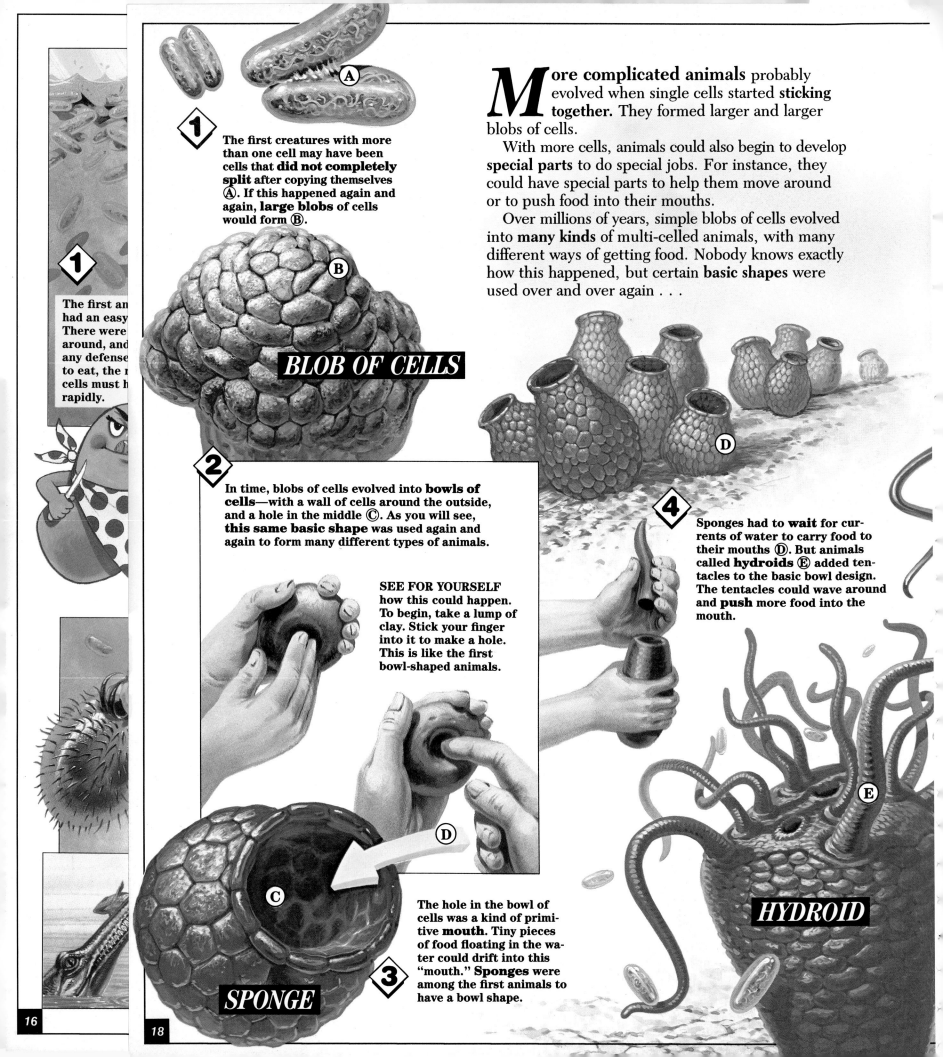

1

The first creatures with more than one cell may have been cells that **did not completely split** after copying themselves Ⓐ. If this happened again and again, **large blobs** of cells would form Ⓑ.

BLOB OF CELLS

More complicated animals probably evolved when single cells started **sticking together.** They formed larger and larger blobs of cells.

With more cells, animals could also begin to develop **special parts** to do special jobs. For instance, they could have special parts to help them move around or to push food into their mouths.

Over millions of years, simple blobs of cells evolved into **many kinds** of multi-celled animals, with many different ways of getting food. Nobody knows exactly how this happened, but certain **basic shapes** were used over and over again . . .

2

In time, blobs of cells evolved into **bowls of cells**—with a wall of cells around the outside, and a hole in the middle Ⓒ. As you will see, **this same basic shape** was used again and again to form many different types of animals.

SEE FOR YOURSELF how this could happen. To begin, take a lump of clay. Stick your finger into it to make a hole. This is like the first bowl-shaped animals.

4

Sponges had to **wait** for currents of water to carry food to their mouths Ⓓ. But animals called **hydroids** Ⓔ added tentacles to the basic bowl design. The tentacles could wave around and **push** more food into the mouth.

The hole in the bowl of cells was a kind of primitive **mouth.** Tiny pieces of food floating in the water could drift into this "mouth." **Sponges** were among the first animals to have a bowl shape.

3

SPONGE

HYDROID

The first an[imals] had an easy [...] There were [...] around, and [...] any defense[s ...] to eat, the [...] cells must h[...] rapidly.

1

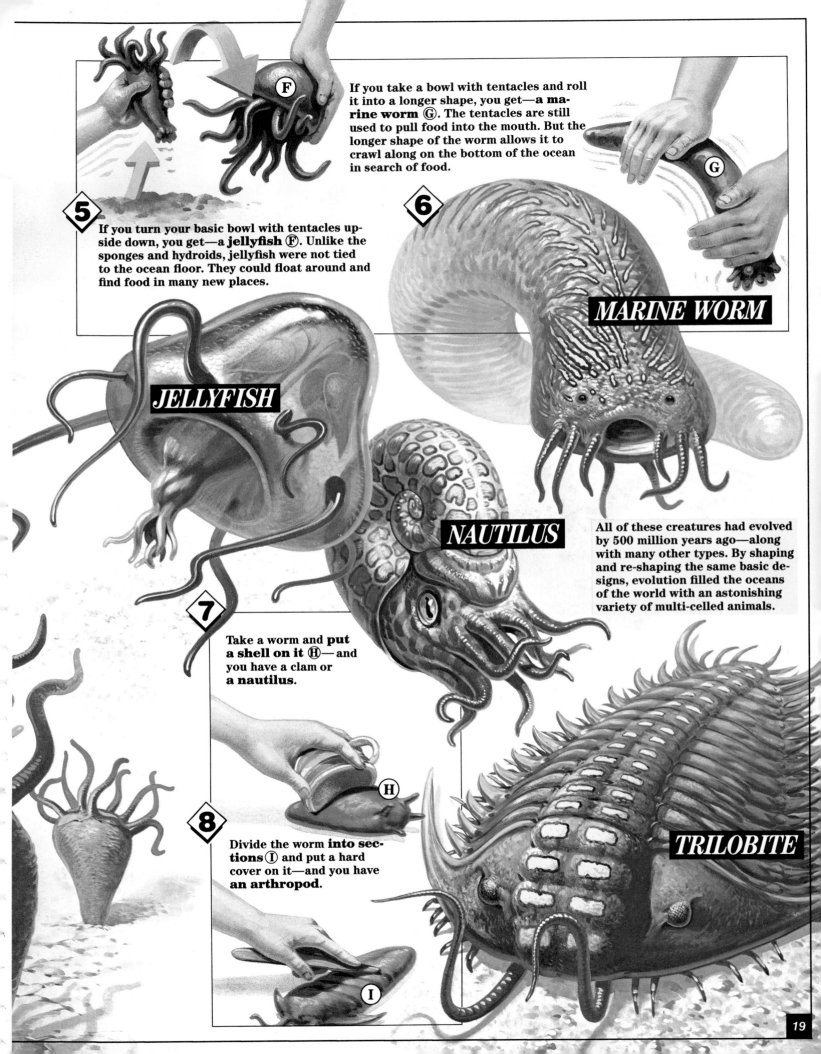

If you take a bowl with tentacles and roll it into a longer shape, you get—**a marine worm** Ⓖ. The tentacles are still used to pull food into the mouth. But the longer shape of the worm allows it to crawl along on the bottom of the ocean in search of food.

⑤ If you turn your basic bowl with tentacles upside down, you get—**a jellyfish** Ⓕ. Unlike the sponges and hydroids, jellyfish were not tied to the ocean floor. They could float around and find food in many new places.

⑥

MARINE WORM

JELLYFISH

NAUTILUS

All of these creatures had evolved by 500 million years ago—along with many other types. By shaping and re-shaping the same basic designs, evolution filled the oceans of the world with an astonishing variety of multi-celled animals.

⑦ Take a worm and **put a shell on it** Ⓗ— and you have a clam or **a nautilus.**

⑧ Divide the worm **into sections** Ⓘ and put a hard cover on it—and you have **an arthropod.**

TRILOBITE

*A*nimals find a place in nature *if* they can evolve ways to get enough food, *if* they can avoid being destroyed by predators or other things, and *if* they can make enough copies of themselves. Each new species that evolves will only survive if many members of the species can succeed in doing these things.

The place that each species has in nature is called its niche (NITCH). This includes the kind of place it lives in. It also includes the kind of food it eats, the animals that prey on it, and the opportunities it has to reproduce. There are millions of different niches on earth—and millions of different kinds of plants and animals that live in them.

1 During the millions of years that life has been evolving, many animals have occupied similar niches. When one species dies out, they leave an empty niche Ⓐ. After a time, another species may evolve to fill the niche Ⓑ.

2 Often, animals that live in similar niches have similar body shapes. This is because certain body shapes work best in certain kinds of places. For example, wings are best for flying in the air—so all creatures that fly have them. Bats are mammals, but their wings are very similar to the wings of ancient flying reptiles.

3 Ancient trilobites were hard-shelled arthropods that lived on the ocean floor—and lobsters live the same way today. And that's why they look so similar.

4 Millions of years ago, reptiles called ichthyosaurs (IK-thee-uh-sawrs) swam in the ocean and hunted fish. Today, mammals called porpoises do the same thing. Look how similar their bodies are—including long rows of small, sharp teeth for grabbing slippery fish!

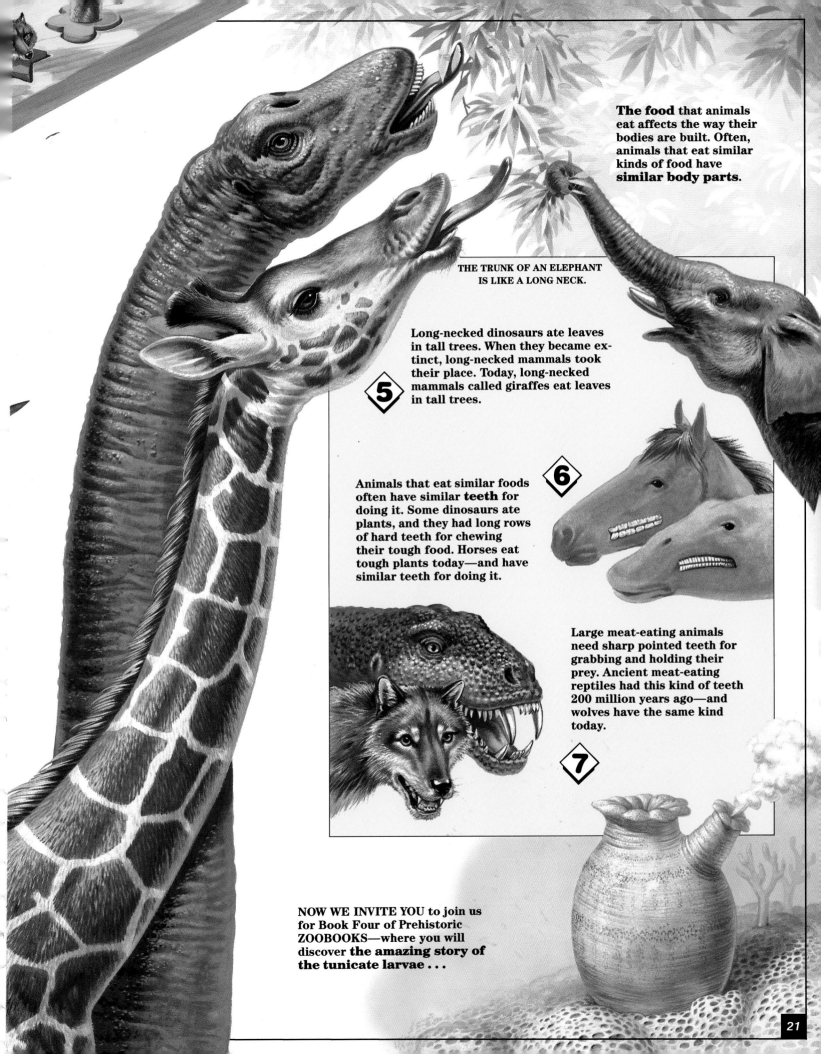

The food that animals eat affects the way their bodies are built. Often, animals that eat similar kinds of food have **similar body parts**.

THE TRUNK OF AN ELEPHANT
IS LIKE A LONG NECK.

Long-necked dinosaurs ate leaves in tall trees. When they became extinct, long-necked mammals took their place. Today, long-necked mammals called giraffes eat leaves in tall trees.

5

Animals that eat similar foods often have similar **teeth** for doing it. Some dinosaurs ate plants, and they had long rows of hard teeth for chewing their tough food. Horses eat tough plants today—and have similar teeth for doing it.

6

Large meat-eating animals need sharp pointed teeth for grabbing and holding their prey. Ancient meat-eating reptiles had this kind of teeth 200 million years ago—and wolves have the same kind today.

7

NOW WE INVITE YOU to join us for Book Four of Prehistoric ZOOBOOKS—where you will discover **the amazing story of the tunicate larvae** . . .

REMEMBER:

1 For many millions of years after life began, the only living things were **simple cells** that lived in the water. They stayed alive by **feeding on chemicals** in the water.

2 The supply of chemicals was limited, and this limited the number of cells. Before life could evolve any further, **a new supply of food was needed.**

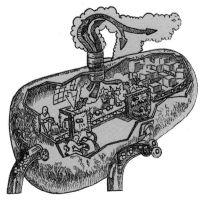

3 Plants developed **a way to make food** from materials that are very common on earth. This way is a process called **photosynthesis.**

4 With a good supply of food, plants were able to evolve into many **different kinds of cells.** And some of the different kinds of cells probably joined together to make **more complicated cells.**

5 Simple cells made copies of themselves by just splitting into two parts. More complicated cells **worked together** to make a copy that was partly like each of them. They were the first "parents" that had a "child."

6 The "child" cell was partly like its "mother" and partly like its "father." This worked so well that many plants and animals have continued to make copies of themselves in this way.

7 At some point, certain types of cells started to eat plants. They became **the first plant-eating animals.** Later on, some other cells started to eat plant-eating cells. They were **the first meat-eating animals.**

8 The plants and animals became part of **a food chain.** The first link of the chain was **the plants.** They were the only living things that could **make food** from chemicals and sunlight.

9 The next link of the chain was **the animals that ate plants.** They are called **herbivores.**

10 The last link of the chain was **the animals that ate other animals.** They are called **carnivores.** Since animals could not make food like plants they **depended totally on plants** to stay alive.

11 To keep from being eaten, plants and animals developed **defenses.** Some "invented" shells and coats of spiny armor. Others simply **grew bigger**, so it was harder for anything to eat them.

NEW WORDS:

Cell membrane:
The skin of a cell. Primitive cells absorbed food from the water around them directly through their cell membranes.

Photosynthesis
(foto-SIN-thuh-sis): The way that some plants use energy from sunlight to turn simple chemicals into food.

Herbivores
(URB-uh-vorz): Animals that eat plants.

12 The way that plants and animals grew bigger was simple—single cells **joined together** to make clumps of cells.

13 Some clumps of cells had a hole in the middle. This was **the first mouth**.

14 Some cells formed into special body parts that **did special jobs**. The arms of a hydroid, for example, worked to catch food and put it in the mouth. As time went on, cells formed many kinds of groups—many kinds of **larger animals and plants**.

15 All the new animals and plants took **different places in nature**. They lived in special areas and ate special kinds of food. **The kind of place** that each plant and animal takes in nature is called its **niche**.

Carnivores
(CAR-nuh-vorz): Animals that eat other animals.

Food Chain:
When plants make food, and the plants are eaten by herbivores, and the herbivores are eaten by carnivores.

Niche (NITCH):
The place that an animal or plant has in nature—the kind of area it lives in, the food it eats, the predators that may eat it.

Index